Lara Lempert

LITVAK
CUISINE

D1430737

baltos lankos

JEWISH CUISINE

Jewish cuisine everywhere formed under the influence of the basic Biblical principle of *kashrut* (Hebrew *kasher* means "appropriate, suitable"). *Kashrut* stipulates the acceptable types of food, the ways of its preparation and consumption, and even the choice of tableware. For example, the meat of non-herbivore, non-cloven-hoofed, and non-ruminating animals is forbidden (the most prominent domestic peculiarity of the Jews in Europe was the refusal to eat pork). Also forbidden is the meat of birds of prey, fish with no scales, fins, or gills (e.g., sheatfish, eels, sturgeon), seafood, marine mammals (whales, dolphins, seals), reptiles, amphibians, and insects, as well as the products of the forbidden animals (e.g., milk, fat, eggs, caviar).

Meat and dairy products must not be mixed not just during preparation, but also in the same meal. Meat products may be eaten an hour after dairy products, while dairy products may be eaten six hours after meat. Meat and dairy products must not be put on the same table. The kitchenware for meat and dairy products, pots to knives to plates, must be separate and kept in different places; they are also washed separately and wiped with different towels.

Products that are neither meat nor dairy (like fish, fruit, and vegetables) make up the category of *parve*. This food may be combined with both meat and dairy dishes.

However, even permitted food is only suitable for food when prepared correctly. First of all, the animal or bird must be slaughtered in a certain way by a specialist called the *shochet*. The rules require minimum torment to be caused to the animal, both out of compassion for every living thing and because fear and suffering can evoke changes in the animal's organism, rendering it unsuitable for consumption. (This is why Jews are not allowed to eat game.) The *shochet* makes sure that every organ in the animal's body was healthy – only then is it allowed to be eaten. These rules do not apply to fish, anyone may cook it.

Both meat and fish should have all the blood removed prior to cooking, as the Bible strictly prohibits the consumption of blood as well as of anything alive (therefore, e.g., an egg with an embryo cannot be used).

Especially high demands are made for wine, because it is part of every holiday ritual, and it is drunk after a blessing. Only wines and other grape drinks (like brandy) made by Jews are permitted – otherwise there is no certainty that it was not affected at some stage of the production cycle in a way that renders it non-kosher. This does not apply to non-grape drinks.

The Jewish cuisine of various regions differs notably and is full of local features, but the rules of *kashrut* are common for all the Jews, regardless of where they live.

Of course, today many Jews are secular and do not keep *kashrut*. However, the traditional Jewish cuisine, including that of Lithuania, follows its directions strictly.

EVERYDAY CUISINE

The everyday cuisine of the Litvaks was not particularly varied in terms of products. Since the 17th century the economic position of the Lithuanian Jewish communities was unstable, and the lifestyle of their members rather modest. The geographical and natural features of the country added to that: even the cuisine of other Lithuanian ethnicities is not extremely diverse, and the Jews additionally excluded pork, game, rabbit, some types of fish. Relatively few Lithuanian Jews engaged in fruit and vegetable gardening, therefore even the local vegetables, herbs, fruit, and berries were used in a limited way in Litvak cuisine. So were forest berries, mushrooms, and nuts, because Jews mostly lived not in villages but in small towns, away from the forest. The most commonly used mushrooms were chanterelles. Spices were rare and expensive in Lithuania, so the Jews mostly used them in holiday dishes, dressing their everyday food with salt, onions and garlic, black or sometimes fragrant pepper (pepper was milled at home by wrapping peppercorns in a cloth and breaking them with a hammer).

Nevertheless, this limited selection of products made up multiple different dishes.

BRAISED HERRING WITH DRIED FRUIT

Cover the bottom of an open braising pot with onion rings and carrot circles, then a layer of dried fruit; top everything with a layer of sliced herring fillet. Pour in water with several tablespoons of sunflower oil to cover the herring. Braise in the oven until the vegetables are ready.

MINCED HERRING

Soak the herring in water, remove the skin and the bones, mince with onion (1 or 2 bulbs per 1 kg herring). Traditionally, a special chopper or a large knife was used for this, but a meat grinder will also do. Grate 1 large sour apple finely, add a little sugar and cinnamon, if you have any. (For want of an apple, some vinegar or lemon juice can be added to the minced herring.) Mix everything, put into an elongated plate, sprinkle with a finely chopped hard-boiled egg.

Braised ▶
herring with
dried fruit

EGG SALAD

Boil eggs, chop finely, mix with chicken grease
and crackling, finely cut onions, and minced garlic
(arbitrary proportions).

MINCED BEEF LIVER

Boil or sauté the liver until ready, run through a meat
grinder together with some onions (1 or 2 per 1 kg
liver). Add the desired amount of chicken or goose
grease to crackling and minced garlic. Instead of
grease and crackling, sunflower seed oil and finely cut
fried onion can be used (do not add the fresh onions
then).

Egg ▶
salad

Milk soup with chanterelles

Finely cut ½ kg well-cleaned and washed mushrooms, 1 carrot, and 1 onion. Cook in ½ litre of water for 30 minutes. Add ½ litre of milk and two potatoes cut into sticks, cook until potatoes are ready. Turn off the fire, add 30 g butter.

Chicken broth with "farfelekh" or "trifelekh" (dough dumplings)

Pour cold water over the prepared and cut chicken (1 kg), put 1 whole peeled carrot and 1 whole peeled onion into the pot, cook covered on a low fire until the meat is cooked, add salt to taste. Remove the meat, the onion, and the carrot from the broth (discard the vegetables), strain it, boil again, and cook the "farfelekh" or "trifelekh" in it.

"Farfelekh". Sift 100–120 g flour into a pile, fold in 1–2 eggs, add salt, knead into dough and form tiny dumplings.

"Trifelekh". Knead 60 g sifted flour and 1 egg into dough (it should be of a pancake consistency, but do not add water). Let out half a teaspoon-full into the broth at a time.

Milk ▶ soup with chanterelles

Duck with kasha (boiled buckwheat) stuffing

Wash the bird, cut off the legs, the head, and the neck, eviscerate. Boil the buckwheat until half ready (100–200 g buckwheat per 1 kg bird), mix with chicken crackling and 1 finely chopped and fried onion, add salt, black pepper, and several cloves of ground or minced garlic. Stuff the bird thoroughly and stitch it up. Stew in a small amount of water in the oven. When the bird is ready, remove the thread, cut, and serve with the stuffing on the side.

Kugel (potato casserole)

Grate 1 kg potatoes finely, add 1–2 finely chopped fried onions, 1 cup of chicken crackling, 2 eggs, stir thoroughly. Grease a pan or a casserole well, lay out the potato paste, bake in the oven until ready.

Duck with ▶
kasha
stuffing

HOLIDAY CUISINE

Most holiday dishes are attributed to the traditional holidays of the Jewish calendar. The features and symbols of the holidays have determined the features of the dishes prepared. For example, by the arrival of *shabbat* (Sabbath), that is, on Friday night, 2 *chalas* (rich white buns) must be baked by the hostess in memory of Biblical events. Food for the Sabbath dinner is prepared so that the laws of this day will not be violated: e.g., the custom of serving stuffed (i.e., boneless) fish is based on the prohibition to separate the fit from the unfit on *shabbat*, including bones from meat. The prohibition to light a fire on *shabbat* has led to the tradition of having cholent, a hot dish of meat and vegetables, for Saturday lunch: on Friday afternoon it was placed in the oven, which was kept on for the day, and by lunch on Saturday the cholent was ready and hot.

For New Year (September–October) Jews try to purchase rare, unusual fruits, so that everyone can try them as a symbol of renewal, and they eat honey, hoping for a "sweet" year. On the eve of Yom Kippur (September–October), the Day of Atonement, nutritious, but not thirst-provoking dishes are served, because this is a fast day when even drinking water is prohibited.

The winter holiday of Hanukkah (December–January) is based on the legend that a single sealed jug of olive oil for the temple lamp was found in the desecrated Jerusalem Temple, but this oil miraculously burned for 8 days until new oil was delivered. In memory of this, oily fried dishes are eaten on Hanukkah – Eastern European Jews usually make potato pancakes.

On Purim, which commemorates the liberation of the Persian Jews from their opressor Haman, described in the Biblical Book of Esther, triangular *homentashen* pies are baked – "Haman's purses".

On Pesach (March–April), the holiday of the Jewish Exodus from slavery in Egypt, yeasty bread is prohibited for a whole week, *matza* (flat bread made of flour and water) is eaten instead, and there must be no leavened products on the table for the week.

The family holiday with the richest culinary tradition is the wedding. The traditional wedding feast was prepared by more than one lady; numerous appetizers, hot dishes, and desserts were served.

Challah

Mix half a cup vegetable oil, 3 teaspoons of salt, 1 tablespoon of sugar, 1 cup hot boiled water, add half a cup cold water and mix again. Dissolve 40–50 g yeast in a 1/3 cup warm water, whip in 3 eggs (leaving several teaspoons of whipped egg to smear the challah), and add to the other ingredients. Pour in 4–5 cups of flour and knead a thin dough. Continue kneading on a board until the dough stops sticking to the hands (add flour if necessary). Put the dough into a bowl, cover with a napkin, and keep for 1 minute in a warmed up (but not hot) oven. Remove, leave for an hour in a warm place (the dough must double in size). Knead on a board again, then divide into 4 parts, and then divide each into 3–4 more. Form the smaller parts into elongated rolls, braid them into 4 challas, set onto a greased baking tray, and leave to rise for 15 minutes. Then smear the challas with the whipped egg, sprinkle with poppyseed, and bake for 30–40 minutes in a preheated oven at medium temperature. Once baked, remove the challas and wrap in napkins or towels. Unwrap in 10–15 minutes and let cool.

GEFILTE FISH (STUFFED FISH)

Clean and eviscerate a large whole fish (carp, pike, or cod), cut it into pieces of 2 centimeters. Remove the head, wash it, cut out the eyes and the gills. Separate the flesh carefully, keeping the skin, and take the bones out. Put the fillet through a meat grinder with 70–100 g onion, add 50 g white bread, soaked in milk and pressed, whip in 1–2 eggs (depending on the size of the fish), add salt, and pepper generously. Fill the skin and the head of the fish with the stuffing; if there is extra stuffing, shape it into balls. Lay out onion rings, beet slices (30–50 g), and carrot circles (1–2 carrots) on the bottom of a large pot, add several laurel leaves and black peppercorns. Place the fish pieces and the balls on the vegetables, pour cold water almost to the top. Wash the bones and gills, put them in a gauze bag and in the pot. Boil half covered for 1½ hours on a low fire (the water must not boil up). Put the boiled pieces of fish out onto a deep elongated dish along with the head and the tail, in the shape of a whole fish with the meatballs on the sides. Decorate the dish with the beet and carrots you boiled with the fish. Strain the broth and pour it over the fish, let it cool. Concentrated fish broth ought to cool quickly.

CHOLENT

Put 1 kg medium pieces of beef brisket together with 80–100 g grease or oil into a large stewing pot with a thick bottom, add salt and pepper, sprinkle with a mixture of finely chopped onions and garlic (enough for the meat to be fully covered), top with 1 large sliced carrot, 2 kg cut up potatoes, add salt, and sprinkle with the onions and garlic as well. Add prunes or raisins to taste, then pour in water over all the ingredients. If there is still room in the pot, you can add several washed raw eggs in their shells. Cholent is best cooked in a stove on a slow fire for 16 to 24 hours.

If you are cooking it in the oven, leave it on a slow fire for no less than 6 hours. The potatoes and the eggs, once peeled, must be brown.

Latkes (potato pancakes)

Peel 1 kg potatoes, grate with a fine grater, whip
in 1 egg, salt. Fry on a well-heated pan. Once the
pancakes are ready, put them into a bowl and keep
in the pre-heated oven for 15 minutes.

Tzimes

Cut 1 kg peeled carrots into sticks, roll in flour, put in
a pot with 50 g raisins, 200 g prunes, 60–100 g sugar,
100 g butter, pour in ½ glass of water. Stew on a slow
fire until the carrots are ready.

Latkes ▶
(potato
pancakes)

Peysakhdike kneydlekh (matza balls)

Put the matzas through a meat grinder once or twice, until the resultant flour is fine enough. Into 2½ cups of flour, whip 2 eggs, 4 tablespoons vegetable oil or chicken grease, add salt and black pepper, cover in cold water, stir, and leave for an hour. Form small balls with wet hands, boil them for 7–10 minutes in water or chicken broth. Kneydlekh can be made with a *neshome* – a "soul", that is, with onions, fried in sunflower seed oil (if made not on Pesakh itself, some dried and finely ground breadcrumbs can be added to the onions). Kneydlekh with *neshome* are made somewhat bigger and boiled for 10–12 minutes.

HOMENTASHN

Make a soft dough from yeast, sifted flour, salt, sugar, vegetable oil, and butter, knead until it stops sticking to the hands. Cover with a warm cloth and keep awhile in a warm place, protected from draughts. Prepare the stuffing: pour boiling water over 150 g poppyseed and cook for 5 minutes, dry off in a gauze-covered colander or sieve. Then put through a meat grinder, add 150 g sugar, stir, and grind once or twice again. Cut the dough into small pieces, roll each piece out, put some stuffing on it, and stick up in a triangular shape. Bake in a hot oven until brown.

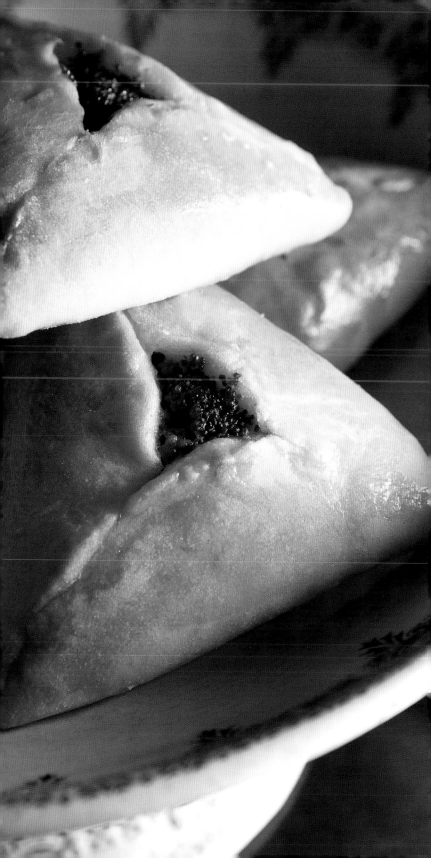

IMBERLEKH (GINGER SWEETS)

Peel, wash, and finely grate 1 kg carrots, mix with 1 kg sugar, 100 g lemon rind. (If the rind is fresh grate it with a fine grater, if it's dried boil it for 15 minutes, let cool, and put through a meat grinder.) Boil the mixture over a small fire in a closed pot until all the liquid is soaked in. Then add 200 g crushed walnuts or almonds, and 2 teaspoons ginger. Set the resulting paste out on a moist board, form a level layer using a wet spoon, and leave aside for 10–12 hours. When the paste sets, cut it into squares, flip them, let dry for 2–3 days, flipping periodically.

TEYGLEKH (HONEY SWEETS)

Whip 6 eggs, add 40 g vegetable oil, pour in 3 cups
sifted flour. Knead a dough of medium thickness
without adding water, divide it into several parts,
forming them into various shapes – stars, circles etc.
Pour 3 cups water, 2 cups honey, and 2 cups sugar
into a deep pot with a sealable lid, stir, and put on the
fire. Once the syrup boils, put the dough shapes in it
quickly, re-seal, and boil on a medium fire for 40–45
minutes. The lid can only be removed for a second,
to stir quickly. Take out the ready teyglekh (they
should be brown) one by one using a skimmer, put
onto a moistened board, sprinkle with sugar or ground
poppyseed.

LEKEKH

Cook a syrup out of 1 cup honey, 1 cup sugar, and
1 cup water (or use the syrup from the teyglekh; in
that case, after the teyglekh are removed, half a liter
kefir is added and stirred without ever letting the syrup
crystallize).

Once the syrup has cooled, pour in 3 tablespoons
vegetable oil, whip in 2 eggs, add ½ teaspoon soda,
stir, add a little flour to make a dough of a cream-like
quality. Pour it into a tall-sided mold, making sure the
dough only fills half of it. Bake in a pre-heated oven
until the lekekh rises to twice its original size.

FRUIT OR BERRY LIQUEUR

Wash the berries or fruit (cherries, cherry plums, plums, raspberries, bilberries, red or black currants), remove the stones if there are any, cover with boiled water. Fill the bottles with berries or fruit of the same kind to the very neck, then pour enough sugar on top to ensure the fruit doesn't come into contact with air. As the juice comes out, the volume of the fruit diminishes, so sugar must be added constantly. In 2–3 months the volume of the juice and the fruit becomes permanent. Strain off the berries, filter the liquid, pour into bottles, and seal. If you add 50 g alcohol or 100 g vodka per 400 g of the liqueur, you will be able to store it for several years. Blackcurrant juice can be added to any ready liqueur to make it better preserved.

UDK 641.5(=924:474.5)(083)
Le-194

Publication sponsored by the Ministry of Culture of the
Republic of Lithuania

We would like to thank Mira Traubienė for her practical advices

Front cover: Imberlekh
Photo © Liudas Masys

Material prepared by:
LARA LEMPERT (author)
OLGA LEMPERT (translation to English)
JOSEPH EVERATT (editor)
DALIA ŠIMAVIČIŪTĖ (series design)
AUDRIS ŠIMAKAUSKAS (layout)
LIUDAS MASYS (photographer)
PATRICIJA JURKŠAITYTĖ (stylist)
MIRA TRAUBIENĖ (consultant and cook)

"Baltos lankos" publishers
Kęstučio St. 10, LT-08116 Vilnius
www.baltoslankos.lt
leidykla@baltoslankos.lt
Printed by "Logotipas"
Utenos St. 41a, LT-08217 Vilnius

2000 copies

Printed in Lithuania
ISBN 978-9955-23-190-5
ISSN 1822-6965